THE PSYCHOLOGY OF
MONEY

WHY YOUR BRAIN CONTROLS YOUR WALLET

DAMI JOSH

Copyright © 2024 by Dami Josh

TABLE OF CONTENT

INTRODUCTION

Welcome to "The Psychology of Money: Why Your Brain Controls Your Wallet," an exploration of the intricate relationship between the human mind and the complex world of finance. In this compelling journey, we delve into the profound ways in which our psychological intricacies influence every financial decision we make. Money is not just a tool; it's a mirror reflecting the depths of our emotions, fears, and aspirations.

As an author deeply immersed in the realms of both psychology and finance, I aim to unravel the mysteries behind our financial behaviors. Drawing from the latest research in behavioral economics, neuroscience, and psychology, this book is a roadmap through the labyrinth of financial decision-making. Why do some individuals consistently make sound financial choices while others are driven by impulse and emotion? What role does our evolutionary history play in shaping our attitudes toward money? These are the questions at the heart of this exploration.

From the primal instincts that drive our spending habits to the cognitive biases that cloud our investment decisions, "The Psychology of Money" is a comprehensive guide to understanding the forces at play within our minds and wallets. Through real-life anecdotes, case studies, and expert insights, readers will gain a profound understanding of the psychological factors that underpin financial success or failure.

Whether you are a seasoned investor, a financial novice, or simply curious about the inner workings of the mind and money, this book offers valuable insights that transcend traditional financial advice. Prepare to embark on a transformative journey that will not only reshape your approach to money but also provide a deeper understanding of yourself and the world of finance. Welcome to a new paradigm in financial literature—one that recognizes the powerful influence of the human psyche on the wealth of nations and individuals alike.

CHAPTER 1: THE EVOLUTIONARY ROOTS OF FINANCIAL BEHAVIOR

Welcome to Chapter 1 of "The Psychology of Money: Why Your Brain Controls Your Wallet." In this segment, we embark on an intriguing exploration into the deep recesses of human evolution to unearth the profound roots of our financial behaviors. Just as our species has evolved physically and intellectually, so too has our relationship with money evolved, shaped by the challenges and opportunities encountered by our ancestors.

In "The Evolutionary Roots of Financial Behavior," we venture into the ancestral landscapes where the seeds of our financial instincts were sown. From the hunter-gatherer societies that thrived on cooperation and resource-sharing to the dawn of agriculture, where concepts of ownership and exchange began to emerge, we unravel the evolutionary tapestry that has woven our modern financial psyche.

Through this journey, we will uncover the survival mechanisms that have subtly sculpted our approach to wealth and resources. How did the scarcity mindset evolve as a survival advantage, and how does it manifest in our contemporary financial decisions? What role did cooperation and social bonds play in the development of trust, a cornerstone of economic transactions?

As we delve into the evolutionary origins of financial behavior, we aim not only to understand the "why" behind our financial choices but also to appreciate the adaptive advantages and pitfalls that have persisted through millennia. Join me as we traverse the landscapes of human evolution, deciphering the genetic code that influences our financial DNA and gaining insights that will illuminate the motivations driving our present-day financial decisions. Welcome to a journey through time, where the echoes of our ancestors resonate in the patterns of our financial behavior today.

Unraveling the primitive instincts that govern our financial decisions

Unravelling the primitive instincts that govern our financial decisions is a multifaceted process that involves delving into the deep recesses of human evolution, psychology, and behavioral economics. This journey is essential to understanding the roots of our financial behaviors and the instinctual impulses that guide our decision-making processes.

1. **Evolutionary Psychology Framework:**

   - Begin by adopting an evolutionary psychology framework, examining how our ancestors' survival and reproductive challenges shaped their behaviors, including those related to resource acquisition and management.

2. Scarcity Mindset Examination:

- Investigate the concept of the scarcity mindset, a primal instinct rooted in our ancestors' struggle for survival. Understand how this mindset influences contemporary financial decisions, often leading to behaviors like hoarding or risk aversion.

3. The Role of Stress and Anxiety:

- Explore the impact of stress and anxiety on financial decision-making. Uncover how our ancestors' experiences with environmental threats and uncertainties contributed to the development of stress responses, influencing present-day financial anxieties and risk perceptions.

4. Cooperation and Social Bonds:

- Examine the evolutionary advantages of cooperation and social bonds in human societies. Understand how the need for collaboration and trust among individuals in ancient communities laid the foundation for economic exchange and transactions.

5. **Neuroscientific Insights:**

   - Integrate insights from neuroscience to understand the neural mechanisms associated with financial decision-making. Investigate how the brain's reward and threat systems, evolved for survival, play a role in our responses to financial gains and losses.

6. **Inherited Behavioral Traits:**

   - Identify specific behaviors and traits that might have been advantageous for survival in ancestral environments and explore how these have been passed down through generations, influencing our financial instincts today.

7. **Comparative Studies:**

   - Compare human financial behaviors with those of other species to gain a broader perspective on the evolutionary roots of economic decision-making. Investigate similarities and differences in how various species manage resources and make economic choices.

8. Application to Modern Context:

- Bridge the gap between ancient instincts and modern financial landscapes. Analyze how the evolutionary roots of our financial behaviors align with or diverge from the challenges and opportunities presented by contemporary economic systems.

By meticulously unravelling these layers, we gain a comprehensive understanding of the primitive instincts that govern our financial decisions. This knowledge provides a solid foundation for developing strategies to navigate the complexities of modern financial environments and make more informed, adaptive choices.

How our ancestral past influences modern spending and saving habits

Our ancestral past exerts a profound influence on modern spending and saving habits, shaping the way we manage resources and make financial decisions in contemporary times. Understanding these influences provides valuable insights into the roots of our behaviors and can guide efforts to navigate the challenges of a complex and often unpredictable economic landscape.

1. **Scarcity Mindset:**

   - Ancestral environments were characterized by scarcity and uncertainty. The scarcity mindset, developed as a survival strategy, compels individuals to prioritize immediate needs over long-term goals. In the modern context, this can manifest in impulsive spending and difficulty in saving for the future.

2. **Risk Aversion:**

- Our ancestors faced real and immediate threats to survival. As a result, risk aversion became a crucial instinct to mitigate potential dangers. In the financial realm, this instinct may translate into a preference for safer, low-risk options, even if they offer lower returns.

3. **Social Hierarchies and Status:**

- Social structures in ancestral communities emphasized hierarchies and status. Acquiring resources, such as valuable possessions, contributed to an individual's standing within the community. This drive for social status continues to influence modern spending habits, with conspicuous consumption serving as a means to display wealth and elevate social standing.

4. Delayed Gratification and Future Planning:

- In environments where resources were unpredictable, individuals who could delay gratification and plan for the future had a survival advantage. This ability to think ahead and save for later is reflected in modern financial behaviors, where successful savers often exhibit patience and a capacity for long-term planning.

5. Cooperative Strategies:

- Ancestors who engaged in cooperative behaviors and shared resources had higher chances of survival. This cooperative instinct has translated into modern financial habits, such as joint financial planning within families or partnerships, reflecting the advantages of collaboration in achieving financial goals.

6. Herd Mentality:

- Ancestral communities relied on cooperation and shared knowledge for survival. This gave rise to a herd mentality, where individuals tended to follow the behaviors of the group. In the modern context, this can be observed in trends such as consumer fads and investment bubbles.

7. **Emotional Responses to Gain and Loss**:

   - Ancestral survival often depended on responding effectively to gains (opportunities) and losses (threats). These emotional responses, wired into our brains over millennia, influence modern financial decisions, with individuals experiencing joy or fear based on financial outcomes.

Understanding how our ancestral past influences spending and saving habits provides a framework for developing strategies to navigate the challenges of modern financial decision-making. By recognizing the evolutionary roots of our behaviors, individuals can work towards aligning their financial choices with their long-term goals and adapting to the demands of the contemporary economic landscape.

The adaptive advantages and pitfalls of our evolutionary financial psychology

The evolutionary financial psychology that has shaped our behaviors around money exhibits both adaptive advantages and pitfalls, reflecting the complex interplay between ancient survival instincts and the demands of modern financial environments.

Adaptive Advantages:

1. Scarcity Mindset:

   - **Advantage:** The instinct to prioritize immediate needs over long-term goals (scarcity mindset) helped our ancestors survive in environments with unpredictable resource availability. In the modern world, this mindset can drive individuals to address pressing financial concerns promptly.

2. Risk Aversion:

- **Advantage:** An inherent aversion to risk was advantageous in environments where miscalculations could lead to dire consequences. This risk aversion can contribute to financial prudence, promoting careful consideration before making investment decisions.

3. Social Cooperation:

- Advantage: Ancestral communities thrived on social cooperation, and individuals who engaged in collaborative behaviors had a survival advantage. This cooperative instinct can manifest positively in modern financial settings, encouraging joint financial planning, partnerships, and community support.

4. Delayed Gratification:

- **Advantage:** The ability to delay gratification and plan for the future provided a significant advantage in environments where resources were unpredictable. This trait continues to be a valuable asset in modern financial contexts, fostering disciplined saving and investment habits.

5. Emotional Responses:

- **Advantage**: Emotional responses to financial outcomes, such as joy from gains and fear from losses, served as effective motivational tools for our ancestors. In the modern world, these emotional responses can drive individuals to stay vigilant about their financial well-being and make adaptive adjustments.

Pitfalls:

1. Biased Decision-Making:

- **Pitfall:** Cognitive biases that were once adaptive can lead to biased decision-making in modern financial contexts. For example, the tendency to overweight immediate rewards over future gains may result in impulsive spending or suboptimal investment decisions.

2. Overemphasis on Short-Term Gains:

- **Pitfall:** The emphasis on short-term survival in ancestral environments may lead to a myopic focus on immediate gains in the modern financial world. This can hinder the pursuit of long-term financial goals, such as retirement planning or wealth accumulation.

3. Herd Mentality:

- **Pitfall**: While a herd mentality was beneficial for survival in ancestral communities, it can lead to detrimental financial behaviors in modern contexts. Herd behavior may contribute to market bubbles, speculative investing, or following financial trends without critical evaluation.

4. Status-Driven Consumption:

- **Pitfall:** The drive for social status, rooted in ancestral hierarchies, can result in status-driven consumption, where individuals prioritize conspicuous spending to display wealth. This can lead to financial stress and hinder responsible financial management.

5. Inability to Adapt Rapidly:

- **Pitfall:** Evolutionary traits, while adaptive in ancestral environments, may not evolve quickly enough to keep pace with the rapid changes in modern financial systems. This can result in maladaptive responses to novel financial challenges.

Understanding the adaptive advantages and pitfalls of our evolutionary financial psychology provides a nuanced perspective on our financial behaviors. By recognizing these influences, individuals can strive to leverage adaptive advantages while mitigating the pitfalls through informed decision-making, financial education, and mindfulness about the evolving nature of our economic landscape.

CHAPTER 2: THE EMOTIONAL LANDSCAPE OF MONEY

Welcome to the immersive journey into the heart of financial decision-making – Chapter 2: "The Emotional Landscape of Money." In this chapter, we navigate the intricate terrain of our emotions and their profound impact on how we perceive, interact with, and ultimately manage our finances. Money is more than just numbers on a balance sheet; it is deeply entwined with the tapestry of our emotions, influencing every financial decision we make.

In exploring the emotional landscape of money, we embark on a quest to unravel the complex interplay between our emotional responses and financial behaviors. From the exhilarating highs of financial success to the depths of anxiety triggered by economic uncertainty, our emotions are powerful drivers that shape the financial choices we embrace or avoid.

This chapter delves into the psychological underpinnings of our emotional responses to money, seeking to answer fundamental questions: Why does a windfall bring joy, and why does a financial setback trigger fear or stress? How do our emotional reactions impact our spending, saving, and investment decisions? By examining the emotional landscape of money, we gain insights into the motivations and drivers that underlie our financial actions.

Throughout this exploration, real-life stories, psychological research, and practical insights converge to illuminate the various facets of our emotional relationship with money. We will uncover the emotional biases that can lead to both financial triumphs and pitfalls, and we will equip ourselves with the knowledge needed to navigate this intricate landscape with greater mindfulness and intention.

Prepare to delve into the depths of joy and sorrow, excitement and anxiety, as we unravel the emotional threads woven into our financial decisions. Welcome to a chapter that transcends the conventional boundaries of financial literature, recognizing that money, at its core, is a profoundly emotional experience that shapes the very fabric of our lives.

The emotional roller coaster of financial decision-making

The emotional roller coaster of financial decision-making reflects the turbulent journey individuals often experience when navigating the complexities of money management. Emotions play a pivotal role in shaping our financial behaviors, influencing everything from spending habits to investment choices. Understanding this emotional roller coaster is crucial for making informed decisions and developing a resilient approach to financial well-being.

1. Joy and Elation:

- Financial success, whether it's a salary increase, a successful investment, or achieving a financial goal, triggers feelings of joy and elation. These positive emotions can reinforce sound financial habits and motivate individuals to continue making prudent decisions.

2. Fear and Anxiety:

- Financial setbacks, market downturns, or unexpected expenses can evoke fear and anxiety. The fear of financial instability may lead to irrational decisions, such as selling investments hastily or avoiding necessary financial planning. Understanding and managing these emotions is vital to prevent impulsive reactions.

3. Guilt and Regret:

- Unwise financial choices or missed opportunities may result in feelings of guilt and regret. Whether it's overspending, making a poor investment, or neglecting savings, these emotions can be powerful motivators for behavioral change but can also hinder progress if not addressed constructively.

4. **Excitement and Impulsivity:**

- Excitement about new financial opportunities or trends can lead to impulsive decision-making. The allure of quick gains or the fear of missing out (FOMO) may drive individuals to make financial choices without thorough consideration, potentially exposing them to unnecessary risks.

5. Contentment and Complacency:

- Periods of financial stability and contentment can breed complacency. While a sense of security is valuable, becoming too comfortable may lead to neglecting financial planning or failing to adapt to changing circumstances. It's essential to strike a

balance between contentment and continued
diligence.

6. Stress and Overwhelm:

- The sheer complexity of financial decision-
making, coupled with external pressures, can induce
stress and overwhelm. Balancing budgets,
managing debt, and planning for the future can be
daunting tasks, and the emotional toll of these
challenges can affect overall well-being.

7. Hope and Optimism:

- Even in the face of financial adversity,
individuals may experience hope and optimism.
Believing in the possibility of financial recovery or
improved circumstances can be a powerful
motivator, encouraging individuals to persevere
through challenges and work towards positive
outcomes.

8. Depression and Despair:

- Prolonged financial difficulties or significant losses may lead to feelings of depression and despair. Coping with the emotional toll of financial struggles requires a holistic approach, involving both financial and mental well-being strategies.

Recognizing and managing this emotional roller coaster is essential for making rational financial decisions. Cultivating emotional intelligence, developing coping mechanisms for stress, and maintaining a balanced perspective on financial successes and setbacks contribute to a healthier and more resilient approach to the emotional landscape of financial decision-making. By acknowledging the highs and lows of this journey, individuals can navigate the emotional roller coaster with greater mindfulness and emerge with a more stable and adaptive financial mindset.

Understanding the impact of fear, greed,

and other emotions on financial choices

Understanding the impact of fear, greed, and other emotions on financial choices is a nuanced process that involves delving into the intricate interplay between psychology, decision-making, and financial behavior. Emotions can profoundly influence how individuals perceive, evaluate, and act on financial information, and recognizing these emotional triggers is essential for making informed and rational choices.

1. Identification of Emotional Triggers:

- The first step in understanding the impact of emotions on financial choices is identifying the specific emotional triggers. Fear often arises in response to perceived threats or uncertainties, while greed may emerge when individuals are enticed by the prospect of significant gains. Other emotions, such as excitement, anxiety, or overconfidence, can also play roles in financial decision-making.

2. Exploration of Past Experiences:

- Examining past financial experiences is crucial for understanding the roots of emotional responses. Previous successes or failures can create emotional imprints that shape current financial behaviors. For example, a past financial loss may trigger a heightened sense of fear, influencing risk aversion.

3. Psychological Biases and Heuristics:

- Investigate the psychological biases and heuristics that contribute to emotional decision-making. Cognitive biases, such as loss aversion and anchoring, can amplify the impact of emotions on financial choices. Understanding these biases helps individuals recognize when emotions may be clouding their judgment.

4. Risk Perception and Tolerance:

- Analyze how fear and greed influence perceptions of risk and risk tolerance. Fear tends to amplify the perception of risk, leading to risk aversion, while greed may diminish the perceived risks associated with potentially lucrative opportunities. Balancing these emotions is crucial for maintaining a realistic and sustainable risk strategy.

5. **Market Conditions and External Influences:**

- Consider the impact of market conditions and external influences on emotional responses. Economic downturns, market volatility, or global events can intensify emotional reactions. Recognizing the external factors that contribute to emotional responses allows for a more contextual understanding of financial decision-making.

6. **Emotional Intelligence Development:**

- Cultivate emotional intelligence to better navigate the emotional landscape of financial choices. This involves recognizing and managing one's own emotions and empathizing with the emotions of others. Emotional intelligence enhances self-awareness and promotes more considered and rational decision-making.

7. Behavioral Economics Insights:

 - Leverage insights from behavioral economics, which explores how psychological factors impact economic decisions. Behavioral economics provides frameworks for understanding the irrational aspects of human behavior, offering tools to mitigate the influence of emotions on financial choices.

8. Mindfulness and Reflection:

 - Encourage mindfulness and reflection to create a space between emotions and decisions. By adopting a mindful approach, individuals can become more aware of their emotional states and choose how to respond, rather than reacting impulsively.

9. Financial Education and Planning:

 - Equip individuals with financial education and planning tools to bolster their decision-making processes. Understanding the long-term implications of financial choices and having a well-defined financial plan can mitigate the influence of short-term emotional fluctuations.

10. **Professional Guidance:**

 - Seek professional guidance from financial advisors who can provide objective insights and help individuals navigate emotional biases. Advisors can offer a rational perspective and assist in developing strategies aligned with long-term financial goals.

By systematically navigating these steps, individuals can gain a more comprehensive understanding of how fear, greed, and other emotions influence their financial choices. This awareness lays the foundation for making more intentional, rational, and resilient decisions in the dynamic landscape of personal finance.

Strategies for managing emotions to make more rational and effective financial decisions

Effectively managing emotions is essential for making rational and sound financial decisions. Emotions such as fear, greed, and anxiety can lead to impulsive choices that may not align with long-term financial goals. Implementing strategies to manage these emotions empowers individuals to navigate the complexities of personal finance with greater clarity and resilience.

1. **Develop Emotional Awareness:**

   - The first step in managing emotions is developing awareness. Regularly check in with your emotional state when making financial decisions. Recognize the specific emotions you are experiencing and how they may be influencing your judgment.

2. Create a Financial Plan:

  - Establishing a comprehensive financial plan provides a structured framework for decision-making. Knowing your financial goals, budget, and investment strategy in advance can reduce the impact of impulsive emotions. Regularly revisit and update the plan as circumstances evolve.

3. Set Realistic Expectations:

  - Cultivate realistic expectations about financial outcomes. Understand that markets fluctuate, and financial plans may encounter unexpected challenges. Realistic expectations help mitigate the emotional impact of unforeseen events and foster a more resilient mindset.

4. Diversify Investments:

  - Diversifying investments across different asset classes can help manage risk and reduce the emotional impact of market fluctuations. A well-diversified portfolio is less susceptible to the extreme highs and lows that can trigger emotional responses.

5. Establish Emergency Funds:

- Creating an emergency fund provides a financial safety net, reducing anxiety about unforeseen expenses. Knowing that you have a buffer for emergencies can alleviate stress and allow for more rational decision-making during challenging times.

6. Practice Mindfulness:

- Incorporate mindfulness practices into your routine. Mindfulness techniques, such as meditation or mindful breathing, can help center your mind, reduce stress, and enhance your ability to make decisions from a calmer and more focused state.

7. Utilize Decision-Making Tools:

- Leverage decision-making tools, such as checklists or decision matrices, to guide your financial choices. Having a systematic approach based on predetermined criteria can help counteract impulsive decisions driven by emotional fluctuations.

8. Seek Professional Advice:

- Consult with financial advisors to gain objective insights and guidance. Professionals can offer a detached perspective and help you make decisions aligned with your financial objectives, irrespective of emotional biases.

9. Implement Cooling-Off Periods:

- Introduce cooling-off periods before making significant financial decisions. Taking time to reflect and reconsider allows emotions to subside, enabling a more rational assessment of the situation.

10. Build a Support System:

- Establish a support system with friends, family, or a financial counsellor. Discussing financial concerns with trusted individuals can provide emotional support and alternative perspectives, helping to put financial decisions into context.

11. Focus on Long-Term Goals:

- Keep long-term financial goals in focus. Remind yourself of the bigger picture and the objectives you aim to achieve. This perspective can act as a stabilizing force during periods of heightened emotional intensity.

12. Continuous Learning:

- Engage in continuous financial education. The more you understand the intricacies of personal finance and investment, the more confident and less emotionally driven your decisions are likely to be.

By incorporating these strategies into your approach to financial decision-making, you can cultivate a more resilient and rational mindset. Managing emotions effectively allows you to navigate the emotional roller coaster of financial decisions with greater poise, promoting financial well-being and long-term success.

CHAPTER 3: THE COGNITIVE BIASES THAT SHAPE OUR FINANCES

Welcome to Chapter 3 of our exploration into the intricate realm of financial decision-making: "The Cognitive Biases That Shape Our Finances." In this chapter, we delve into the fascinating world of cognitive biases—deep-seated patterns of thought that can subtly and profoundly influence the choices we make with our money. Understanding these biases is essential for anyone seeking to navigate the complex landscape of personal finance with clarity and informed decision-making.

As we embark on this journey, we will unravel the hidden forces that shape our financial behaviors, often leading us down paths that defy conventional economic reasoning. Cognitive biases, rooted in the quirks of human psychology, can impact everything from investment choices to spending habits, subtly steering us away from optimal financial outcomes.

This chapter goes beyond traditional financial advice, shining a light on the ways our brains can lead us astray. From the tendency to anchor our decisions to irrelevant information to the aversion to perceived losses, we will explore a spectrum of biases that influence our financial judgments. By understanding these biases, we gain a powerful tool for dissecting our thought processes and making financial decisions more aligned with our true objectives.

Through real-world examples, psychological insights, and practical strategies, we will navigate the terrain of cognitive biases that permeate our financial world. This exploration is not just an academic exercise; it is a practical guide for individuals seeking to outsmart their minds and make financial decisions that stand the test of rational scrutiny.

Prepare to challenge your assumptions, question your instincts, and gain a deeper understanding of the cognitive underpinnings that shape the way you handle money. Welcome to a chapter that unveils the invisible threads woven into the fabric of our financial decisions, empowering you to navigate the biases that influence us all.

The cognitive shortcuts and biases that affect our financial judgments

Cognitive shortcuts and biases are inherent aspects of human thinking that can significantly impact financial judgments, often leading to deviations from rational decision-making. Understanding these cognitive patterns is crucial for individuals aiming to make more informed and objective financial choices. Here, we explore some prominent cognitive shortcuts and biases that influence our financial judgments:

1. Anchoring Bias:

- This bias involves relying too heavily on the first piece of information encountered when making decisions. In a financial context, individuals may anchor their judgments based on initial values, such as the purchase price of a stock or the starting point of a negotiation, even if these values are irrelevant to the decision at hand.

2. Confirmation Bias:

- Confirmation bias refers to the tendency to favor information that confirms preexisting beliefs or decisions while ignoring or downplaying conflicting evidence. In finance, individuals may selectively seek information that supports their investment choices, potentially overlooking warning signs or alternative perspectives.

3. Loss Aversion:

- Loss aversion is the inclination to prefer avoiding losses rather than acquiring equivalent gains. In financial decisions, this bias may lead individuals to take on excessive risk to avoid perceived losses, or conversely, to sell winning investments prematurely to secure gains.

4. Overconfidence Bias:

- Overconfidence bias involves an individual's tendency to overestimate their abilities, knowledge, or predictions. In finance, this bias can lead to excessive trading, unwarranted risk-taking, or neglecting the potential for unexpected events that may impact investments.

5. Regency Bias:

- Regency bias occurs when individuals give more weight to recent events when making judgments. In financial contexts, this bias can lead to a disproportionate focus on recent market trends or short-term performance, potentially overlooking the long-term historical context.

6. Availability Heuristic:

- The availability heuristic is the tendency to rely on information readily available in memory when making decisions. In finance, individuals may base judgments on recent news, experiences, or vivid examples, rather than a comprehensive analysis of relevant data.

7. Herding Behavior:

- Herding behavior involves individuals following the actions of the crowd rather than making independent decisions. In finance, this can contribute to market bubbles, as individuals may join the majority in buying or selling assets based on collective sentiment rather than individual analysis.

8. Endowment Effect:

- The endowment effect is the tendency to assign a higher value to things simply because they are owned. In financial decisions, this bias may lead individuals to overvalue their current investments or assets, influencing decisions to buy, sell, or hold based on emotional attachment.

9. Sunk Cost Fallacy:

 - The sunk cost fallacy is the inclination to continue investing in a decision or project based on past investments, despite new information suggesting it may not be the best course of action. In finance, individuals may hold onto losing investments instead of cutting their losses.

10. **Hindsight Bias:**

 - Hindsight bias is the tendency to perceive events as having been predictable after they have already occurred. In finance, individuals may believe they could have predicted market movements or economic events after the fact, leading to overconfidence in future predictions.

Addressing these cognitive shortcuts and biases requires self-awareness, critical thinking, and a commitment to evidence-based decision-making. By recognizing these patterns, individuals can work towards minimizing their impact, making more rational financial judgments, and enhancing their overall financial well-being.

How heuristics impact investment choices and risk assessment

Heuristics, or mental shortcuts, significantly impact investment choices and risk assessment. These cognitive tools are essential for making decisions quickly, especially in complex situations. However, when it comes to investments, heuristics can lead to biases and deviations from rational decision-making. Here's how heuristics influence investment choices and risk assessment:

1. **Representativeness Heuristic:**

   - Investors often use the representativeness heuristic to make judgments based on how closely an investment or situation resembles a prototype. For example, a company with characteristics similar to successful companies in the past may be perceived as a good investment. This can lead to overlooking unique aspects and exaggerating similarities.

2. **Availability Heuristic:**

- The availability heuristic involves relying on readily available information when making decisions. In the context of investments, individuals may give more weight to recent news, media coverage, or events, impacting perceptions of risk and return. This can lead to a focus on short-term trends and a neglect of long-term fundamentals.

3. **Anchoring Heuristic:**

- Anchoring occurs when investors rely too heavily on the first piece of information encountered when making decisions. For example, if an investor hears a particular price target for a stock, this anchor can influence subsequent valuations, potentially leading to overvalued or undervalued assessments.

4. **Regency Bias:**

 - Investors often exhibit a regency bias, emphasizing recent information or trends in decision-making. This can impact risk assessment by causing investors to overreact to short-term market movements, neglecting the long-term historical context of an investment's performance.

5. **Availability Cascade:**

 - Availability cascade occurs when repeated exposure to a particular narrative or idea leads individuals to accept it as true, irrespective of its actual validity. Investment choices can contribute to market bubbles or panics, as investors follow popular narratives without conducting independent analysis.

6. **Overconfidence Bias:**

- Overconfidence bias plays a role in risk assessment by causing investors to overestimate their ability to predict market movements or the success of specific investments. This can lead to excessive trading, unwarranted risk-taking, and inadequate diversification.

7. Familiarity Heuristic:

- Investors often rely on the familiarity heuristic, favoring investments they are familiar with or companies they know well. While familiarity can provide a sense of comfort, it may lead to neglecting other opportunities and inadequate diversification.

8. Herd Behavior:

- Herding behavior is driven by the heuristic of following the crowd. Investors may make investment choices based on the actions of others rather than conducting independent analysis. This can contribute to market trends that deviate from rational valuations.

9. Loss Aversion:

- Loss aversion, while not strictly a heuristic, influences risk assessment by causing investors to be more averse to losses than enticed by equivalent gains. This bias can impact decisions related to selling winning investments prematurely or holding onto losing investments longer than warranted.

10. Sunk Cost Fallacy:

- The sunk cost fallacy, a cognitive bias related to heuristics, influences investment choices by causing investors to consider past investments when evaluating future decisions. This may lead to holding onto an investment based on prior commitments, even when new information suggests a change is warranted.

Understanding how heuristics impact investment choices and risk assessment is essential for investors seeking to make informed and objective decisions. By being aware of these cognitive shortcuts, investors can employ strategies to mitigate their influence, such as diversification, disciplined decision-making, and a focus on long-term fundamentals rather than short-term trends.

Practical techniques to overcome cognitive biases and make better financial decisions

Overcoming cognitive biases is a challenging but crucial endeavor for making better financial decisions. Here are practical techniques to help individuals mitigate the influence of cognitive biases and foster more rational and informed choices:

1. **Awareness and Education:**

 - Begin by educating yourself about common cognitive biases and their impact on decision-making. Awareness is the first step in overcoming biases. Recognize that everyone is susceptible to cognitive errors, and an understanding of these biases lays the foundation for improvement.

2. **Slow and Deliberate Decision-Making:**

- Adopt a slower and more deliberate decision-making process. Taking time to thoroughly analyze information and consider alternative perspectives can help counteract impulsive and biased judgments. Implementing a "cooling-off" period before making significant financial decisions allows emotions to subside.

3. **Diversification and Risk Management:**

- Implement a diversified investment strategy and risk management plan. Diversification helps mitigate the impact of biases associated with individual investments. Having a well-defined risk management strategy can provide a rational framework for handling market fluctuations.

4. **Evidence-Based Decision-Making:**

- Emphasize evidence-based decision-making over intuition. Rely on data, research, and historical trends rather than succumbing to emotional impulses. Develop a disciplined approach that aligns with long-term goals and is grounded in objective analysis.

5. Checklists and Decision Matrices:

- Use checklists and decision matrices to guide financial decisions. Having a systematic approach based on predetermined criteria can help individuals make more objective assessments, reducing the influence of subjective biases.

6. Seek Diverse Perspectives:

- Actively seek diverse perspectives and opinions. Engaging with others who hold different views can provide valuable insights and challenge preconceived notions. This helps counteract biases like confirmation bias by encouraging a more comprehensive evaluation of information.

7. Consult with Trusted Advisors:

- Consult with trusted financial advisors. Professional advice can offer an external, unbiased perspective on financial decisions. Advisors can help individuals navigate cognitive biases and provide guidance aligned with their financial goals.

8. Use Behavioral Prompts:

- Implement behavioral prompts to counteract biases. For example, setting specific rules for buying or selling investments based on predetermined criteria can help individuals adhere to rational decision-making even in the face of emotional pressures.

9. Focus on Long-Term Goals:

- Keep long-term goals in focus. Remind yourself regularly of your broader financial objectives. This perspective can help prioritize decisions that align with your overall financial plan rather than succumbing to short-term emotional fluctuations.

10. Regularly Review and Reflect:

- Establish a habit of regularly reviewing financial decisions and reflecting on outcomes. Analyze both successful and unsuccessful decisions to identify patterns and learn from experiences. This reflective practice contributes to ongoing improvement.

11. Utilize Technology:

- Leverage technology tools that facilitate disciplined decision-making. Automated investment strategies, robo-advisors, and financial apps can help individuals adhere to predetermined plans and reduce the impact of emotional biases.

12. Mindfulness and Emotional Regulation:

- Incorporate mindfulness techniques and emotional regulation practices. Mindfulness helps individuals become more aware of their emotions and reactions, allowing for more conscious decision-making. Techniques such as deep breathing or meditation can contribute to emotional regulation.

By integrating these practical techniques into financial decision-making processes, individuals can enhance their ability to overcome cognitive biases. The goal is to create a more rational, evidence-based approach that aligns with long-term financial objectives and withstands the influences of emotional biases.

CHAPTER 4: THE SOCIAL PSYCHOLOGY OF MONEY

Welcome to the captivating exploration of the intricate dynamics that shape our financial lives – Chapter 4: "The Social Psychology of Money." In this chapter, we venture beyond individual decision-making and delve into the fascinating intersection of money and social behavior. Money is not only a personal asset but also a social force that weaves through the fabric of our relationships, aspirations, and societal structures.

As we embark on this journey, we will unravel the profound influence of social psychology on our financial choices. From the impact of societal norms on spending habits to the role of social comparison in shaping our financial aspirations, we will navigate the rich landscape where money and social dynamics intersect.

This chapter goes beyond conventional financial wisdom, recognizing that money is not just a numerical entity but a complex social construct. Our financial decisions are not made in isolation but are deeply entwined with cultural expectations, peer influences, and societal pressures.

Through the lens of social psychology, we will explore how our relationships, communities, and broader cultural contexts shape our attitudes towards money. Real-life stories, psychological insights, and practical strategies converge to illuminate the various ways in which social factors influence our financial behaviors.

Get ready to unravel the social tapestry woven into our financial decisions. Welcome to a chapter that transcends the traditional boundaries of financial literature, acknowledging that money is as much about people as it is about numbers. Together, let's uncover the social psychology of money and gain a deeper understanding of how our financial lives are intricately woven into the fabric of our social world.

The influence of social norms, peer pressure, and societal expectations on financial behavior

The influence of social norms, peer pressure, and societal expectations on financial behavior is a multifaceted and powerful force that significantly shapes the way individuals manage money. These social factors play a crucial role in shaping spending habits, saving patterns, and overall financial decision-making. Understanding their impact is essential for anyone seeking to navigate the complex interplay between social dynamics and personal finance.

1. Social Norms:

- Social norms are unwritten rules that govern acceptable behavior within a particular social group. In the realm of finance, social norms can dictate what is considered normal or acceptable in terms of spending, saving, and investing. For example, if conspicuous consumption is the norm within a social circle, individuals may feel pressured to conform to these spending patterns.

2. Peer Pressure:

- Peer pressure refers to the influence that individuals within a social group exert on each other to conform to certain behaviors or choices. In the context of finances, peer pressure can lead to spending decisions driven by the desire to fit in or meet the expectations of peers. This pressure may manifest in lifestyle inflation, where individuals increase spending to match the perceived financial status of their peers.

3. Societal Expectations:

- Societal expectations encompass broader cultural and societal norms that influence how individuals perceive success, achievement, and financial well-being. For example, societal expectations may prescribe specific milestones such as homeownership, certain career achievements, or the attainment of a certain lifestyle. These expectations can drive individuals to make financial decisions aligned with societal norms rather than personal values.

4. Conspicuous Consumption:

- Coined by economist Thorstein Veblen, conspicuous consumption refers to the public display of wealth and material possessions as a means of signaling social status. Individuals may engage in conspicuous consumption to meet societal expectations or gain approval within their social circles, even if it means compromising their financial well-being.

5. Financial Envy and Social Comparison:

- Social comparison theory suggests that individuals determine their own social and personal worth based on how they stack up against others. In the financial context, constant exposure to others' financial successes or acquisitions through social media or direct observation can lead to financial envy and drive individuals to make financial decisions to keep up or surpass their peers.

6. Cultural Influences:

- Cultural factors, including traditions, values, and belief systems, play a significant role in shaping financial behaviors. Cultural expectations regarding family responsibilities, generosity, and financial priorities can influence how individuals allocate their resources.

7. Social Networks and Financial Behavior:

- The structure of an individual's social network can impact financial behavior. If close connections prioritize certain financial practices, individuals within the network may be more likely to adopt similar behaviors. This can include investment choices, spending habits, and attitudes toward debt.

8. Financial Education and Literacy within Social Circles:

- The level of financial education and literacy within social circles can influence financial behavior. If financial knowledge is limited within a community, individuals may make decisions based on collective misconceptions or lack of information, reinforcing shared financial behaviors.

Mitigating the Influence:

1. Define Personal Values:

- Clearly define personal values and financial goals. Understanding what matters most to you can help resist external pressures that may conflict with your intrinsic values.

2. Cultivate Financial Literacy:

- Actively pursue financial education and literacy. By gaining a solid understanding of financial principles, individuals can make more informed decisions based on objective information rather than social pressures.

3. **Build a Supportive Financial Community:**

- Surround yourself with a supportive financial community that values prudent financial practices. Shared financial values within a community can provide positive reinforcement and counteract negative societal pressures.

4. **Set Boundaries and Prioritize:**

- Establish personal boundaries and priorities based on your financial goals. This may involve setting limits on discretionary spending or making conscious decisions about the lifestyle you want to lead.

5. **Practice Mindful Spending:**

- Adopt mindful spending habits by regularly assessing whether purchases align with personal values and long-term financial objectives. Mindful spending involves intentional decision-making rather than succumbing to impulsive desires.

6. **Utilize Positive Peer Pressure:**

- Surround yourself with peers who positively influence financial behavior. Positive peer pressure within a supportive network can foster a culture of responsible financial decision-making.

Understanding the influence of social norms, peer pressure, and societal expectations on financial behavior is the first step towards making conscious and empowered choices. By recognizing these influences, individuals can proactively shape their financial narratives, aligning their decisions with personal values and long-term aspirations.

How our relationships and social networks shape our financial choices

Our relationships and social networks play a pivotal role in shaping our financial choices. The influence of family, friends, colleagues, and broader social connections can impact various aspects of our financial behavior. Understanding these dynamics is crucial for individuals seeking to navigate the complex interplay between social relationships and personal finance.

1. **Family Influence:**

   - Family is often one of the most significant influencers of financial behavior. Early experiences and lessons learned within the family unit can shape attitudes toward money, spending habits, and the approach to financial planning. Cultural and generational financial practices may also be passed down, influencing individual choices.

2. Spousal Influence:

- Spouses or life partners can have a profound impact on each other's financial decisions. Collaborative financial goal-setting, communication about spending habits, and joint decision-making contribute to a shared financial approach. Conversely, conflicting financial values can lead to tension and influence individual choices within the partnership.

3. Peer Pressure within Social Circles:

- Friends and colleagues within social circles can exert peer pressure, influencing spending patterns and lifestyle choices. Individuals may be inclined to align their financial behaviors with those of their peers, whether it be in terms of housing choices, travel, or leisure activities.

4. Professional Networks:

- Colleagues and professional networks can influence financial choices, especially in terms of career aspirations, job changes, and lifestyle expectations. Pressure to conform to certain professional standards or participate in specific social activities associated with the workplace can impact spending and saving decisions.

5. Social Media Influence:

- The rise of social media has introduced a new dimension to how relationships shape financial choices. The constant exposure to the financial achievements and lifestyles of others on social platforms can lead to social comparison and influence individual spending patterns and aspirations.

6. Community and Cultural Expectations:

- Communities and cultural groups often have shared expectations and norms regarding financial behavior. Individuals may feel compelled to adhere to these expectations, whether related to housing choices, education, or other significant financial decisions.

7. Financial Support and Dependence:

- Relationships involving financial support, such as parent-child dynamics or financial dependence on a partner, can significantly shape financial choices. Dependence may limit financial autonomy, while support structures can influence investment decisions, educational choices, and overall financial well-being.

8. Inherited Beliefs and Values:

- Inherited beliefs and values from social networks can impact financial choices. Individuals may adopt financial practices and attitudes from their social circles, reflecting shared values and expectations.

Mitigating the Influence:

1. Open Communication:

- Foster open communication about financial values, goals, and concerns within relationships. Transparent discussions with family members, partners, and close friends can create a shared understanding and help align financial choices.

2. Joint Financial Planning:

- Engage in joint financial planning with significant others. Collaboratively setting financial goals, creating budgets, and making investment decisions can ensure that both partners are actively involved in shaping the financial future.

3. Establish Boundaries:

- Establish personal financial boundaries within social circles. While it's essential to participate in social activities, individuals should set limits to align with their financial goals and priorities.

4. Cultivate Financial Literacy:

- Cultivate financial literacy within social networks. Encouraging conversations about financial education and knowledge-sharing within families, friend groups, or communities can empower individuals to make informed choices.

5. Seek Positive Influences:

- Surround yourself with positive financial influences. Seek out relationships and social networks that support responsible financial behavior and share similar values.

6. Independence and Autonomy:

- Foster financial independence and autonomy within relationships. Encourage each partner to maintain a degree of financial independence, allowing for personal financial goals and choices within the context of a shared financial plan.

7. Social Media Awareness:

- Be mindful of the influence of social media. Recognize that curated online personas may not reflect the full financial reality of others. Limiting exposure to content that triggers social comparison can help mitigate its impact.

8. Continuous Reflection:

- Regularly reflect on the influence of relationships on financial choices. Evaluate whether financial decisions align with personal values and goals, and make adjustments as needed.

By being aware of how relationships and social networks shape financial choices, individuals can take proactive steps to navigate these influences effectively. Cultivating open communication, setting boundaries, and fostering financial literacy within social circles contribute to a more informed and empowered approach to personal finance.

Navigating societal pressures to align personal values with financial decisions

Navigating societal pressures to align personal values with financial decisions can be a challenging but rewarding process. Societal expectations, cultural norms, and peer influences often exert significant pressure on individuals to conform to certain financial behaviors. However, aligning personal values with financial choices involves a deliberate and introspective approach. Here's a step-by-step guide to navigating societal pressures:

1. **Define Personal Values:**

   - Begin by clearly defining your values and priorities. What matters most to you in life? This could include factors such as family, personal growth, philanthropy, or experiences.

Understanding your core values provides a foundation for making financial decisions that resonate with your true aspirations.

2. Set Financial Goals:

- Establish specific and measurable financial goals based on your values. Whether it's saving for a meaningful experience, contributing to a cause, or achieving financial independence, having concrete objectives allows you to align your financial decisions with your values.

3. Understand Societal Pressures:

- Gain awareness of the societal pressures and expectations that may influence financial decisions. This includes cultural norms, peer influences, and external expectations regarding lifestyle, consumption, and success. Recognizing these pressures is the first step in navigating them.

4. Evaluate Lifestyle Choices:

- Reflect on your current lifestyle choices and spending patterns. Are they aligned with your values and financial goals, or are they influenced by external pressures? Assessing your lifestyle choices helps identify areas where societal pressures may be impacting your financial decisions.

5. Establish Financial Boundaries:

- Set clear financial boundaries that align with your values. This may involve defining limits on spending, avoiding unnecessary debt, or resisting the urge to conform to societal expectations that don't align with your priorities.

6. Communicate with Loved Ones:

- Engage in open and honest communication with loved ones about your values and financial goals. This is especially important within close relationships where shared financial decisions are involved. Communicating your priorities helps build understanding and support.

7. Seek Like-Minded Communities:

- Connect with communities or groups that share similar values. Whether online or in-person, finding like-minded individuals provides a supportive environment where you can exchange ideas, share experiences, and receive encouragement to stay true to your financial values.

8. Educate Others:

- Take opportunities to educate others about your financial values and choices. This can help dispel misconceptions and reduce external pressures. Sharing your perspective may also encourage others to reconsider their own financial decisions.

9. Practice Mindful Spending:

- Adopt mindful spending habits by consciously evaluating purchases about your values and goals. Ask yourself if a particular expense aligns with your priorities and if it contributes to your long-term aspirations.

10. Prioritize Experiences over Possessions:

- Emphasize experiences over material possessions. Societal pressures often promote a culture of consumerism, but prioritizing meaningful experiences can lead to more fulfilling and value-aligned financial choices.

11. Build a Financial Plan:

- Develop a comprehensive financial plan that integrates your values and goals. This plan should include budgeting, saving, investing, and debt management strategies that align with your overarching priorities.

12. Embrace Financial Independence:

- Strive for financial independence to reduce external dependencies and pressures. Becoming financially independent allows you greater autonomy in making decisions that align with your values without being overly influenced by external expectations.

13. Regularly Reassess and Adjust:

- Periodically reassess your values, goals, and financial decisions. Life circumstances and priorities evolve, and it's essential to adjust your financial plan accordingly. Regular reassessment ensures that your decisions remain in alignment with your evolving values.

Navigating societal pressures to align personal values with financial decisions is an ongoing process that requires self-awareness, resilience, and commitment. By taking intentional steps and fostering a financial mindset rooted in personal values, individuals can shape a financial narrative that authentically reflects their aspirations and priorities.

CHAPTER 5: BUILDING A MINDFUL MONEY MINDSET

Welcome to a transformative exploration into the intricate relationship between mindfulness and personal finance—Chapter 5: "Building a Mindful Money Mindset." In this chapter, we embark on a journey that transcends conventional financial advice, inviting you to cultivate a profound awareness and consciousness in your financial decisions.

In a world inundated with information, distractions, and societal pressures, the concept of mindfulness emerges as a beacon of clarity in the realm of personal finance. Mindful money management is not just about budgets and investments; it is a holistic approach that integrates the principles of mindfulness into every financial choice we make.

As we delve into this chapter, we will unravel the layers of a mindful money mindset—a mindset that goes beyond numbers and embraces a deeper understanding of our values, attitudes, and behaviors concerning money. Drawing from ancient contemplative practices and modern behavioral psychology, we will explore how cultivating mindfulness can transform the way we perceive, manage, and relate to our financial lives.

Through practical exercises, real-life anecdotes, and strategic insights, we will guide you on a path to develop a mindful money mindset that fosters a sense of abundance, gratitude, and conscious decision-making. This chapter serves as a bridge between the ancient wisdom of mindfulness and the practicalities of contemporary finance, empowering you to navigate the complexities of money with clarity, intention, and a renewed sense of purpose.

Prepare to embark on a journey that transcends the traditional boundaries of personal finance literature.

Welcome to a chapter that invites you to pause, reflect, and intentionally shape a mindful money mindset—one that aligns your financial choices with your values and leads to a more fulfilling and harmonious relationship with money.

Cultivating mindfulness to enhance financial awareness

Cultivating mindfulness to enhance financial awareness involves developing a heightened state of present-moment attention and intentional focus on your financial decisions. Mindfulness in the context of personal finance enables you to build a deeper understanding of your values, attitudes, and behaviors related to money. Here's a step-by-step process to help you integrate mindfulness into your financial awareness:

1. **Define Financial Values:**

- Begin by clarifying your financial values. Identify what truly matters to you in terms of money—whether it's financial security, freedom, experiences, or giving back. This foundational step sets the stage for aligning your financial decisions with your core values.

2. Practice Mindful Breathing:

- Incorporate mindfulness meditation techniques, starting with mindful breathing. Take moments throughout your day to focus on your breath, bringing your attention to the present moment. This practice enhances self-awareness and helps you develop the capacity to observe your thoughts and reactions without immediate judgment.

3. Create Financial Mindfulness Rituals:

- Establish specific rituals or routines for financial activities. For example, designate a set time each week to review your budget, analyze spending patterns, or assess your financial goals. These rituals create a structured space for mindful reflection on your financial decisions.

4. Engage in Conscious Spending:

 - Practice conscious spending by bringing mindfulness to your purchases. Before making a financial decision, pause and reflect on whether the expenditure aligns with your values and priorities. This intentional approach fosters awareness and helps you avoid impulsive or emotionally driven spending.

5. Maintain a Financial Journal:

 - Keep a financial journal to document your thoughts, feelings, and reflections on money. This journal serves as a tool for self-discovery and allows you to track patterns in your financial behavior. Regularly reviewing your entries enhances awareness and facilitates conscious decision-making.

6. Practice Gratitude for Financial Well-Being:

 - Cultivate gratitude for your financial well-being, regardless of your current circumstances. Regularly reflect on the positive aspects of your financial life, such as steady income, savings, or the ability to meet basic needs. Gratitude enhances mindfulness by redirecting focus from scarcity to abundance.

7. **Mindful Communication about Finances:**

- Practice mindful communication about finances with your family or financial partners. Engage in open, non-judgmental conversations about financial goals, challenges, and aspirations. Mindful communication fosters understanding and strengthens financial relationships.

8. **Mindful Decision-Making:**

- Apply mindfulness to decision-making by consciously weighing the pros and cons of financial choices. Avoid making decisions impulsively or out of fear. Give yourself the space to reflect on the potential consequences and long-term impact of each decision.

9. **Embrace Financial Challenges Mindfully:**

- Approach financial challenges with mindfulness and resilience. Instead of reacting with stress or anxiety, observe your emotions and thoughts without judgment. Mindful acceptance allows you to respond to challenges with greater clarity and creativity.

10. **Financial Mindfulness Retreats or Courses:**

- Consider participating in financial mindfulness retreats or courses. These programs offer structured guidance and practices specifically designed to integrate mindfulness into your financial life. They provide a supportive environment for cultivating awareness and promoting intentional financial choices.

11. **Regular Self-Reflection:**

- Set aside time for regular self-reflection on your financial journey. Ask yourself questions about your financial goals, progress, and areas for improvement. This self-inquiry deepens your understanding of your relationship with money and reinforces mindful financial habits.

12. **Celebrate Financial Milestones Mindfully:**

- Celebrate financial milestones mindfully by acknowledging your achievements without immediately shifting focus to the next goal. Cultivate a sense of satisfaction and appreciation for your financial progress, fostering a positive and mindful approach to your financial journey.

Integrating mindfulness into your financial awareness is an ongoing process that requires consistent practice and self-reflection. By incorporating these steps into your daily life, you can develop a mindful money mindset that enhances your financial well-being and brings a sense of purpose and clarity to your financial decisions.

Integrating mindfulness techniques for better decision-making and financial well-being

Integrating mindfulness techniques into your decision-making process can significantly enhance financial well-being by fostering greater awareness, reducing impulsive behaviors, and promoting intentional choices. Here's a step-by-step process to help you incorporate mindfulness into your decision-making for better financial outcomes:

1. **Mindful Awareness of Emotions:**

   - Begin by cultivating awareness of your emotions, particularly those related to financial decisions. Take time to recognize and observe any feelings of stress, anxiety, or excitement associated with money. Mindful awareness allows you to detach from emotional reactions and approach decisions with greater clarity.

2. **Mindful Breathing:**

 - Before making financial decisions, engage in mindful breathing exercises. Take a few moments to focus on your breath, allowing it to anchor you in the present moment. This practice helps calm the mind, reduce stress, and create mental space for more deliberate decision-making.

3. **Pause and Reflect:**

 - Incorporate a pause before making significant financial choices. Instead of acting on impulse, intentionally pause and reflect on the decision at hand. This moment of reflection allows you to consider the potential consequences and align the decision with your financial goals.

4. **Body Scan Technique:**

 - Use the body scan technique to bring awareness to physical sensations associated with financial decisions. This involves systematically scanning your body for tension or discomfort. Identifying physical reactions can provide insights into underlying emotions and guide you in making decisions that align with your well-being.

5. Clarify Financial Values:

- Mindfully clarify your financial values and priorities. Reflect on what truly matters to you in the context of money. Understanding your values provides a foundation for making decisions that align with your overarching life goals and aspirations.

6. Mindful Decision-Making Framework:

- Develop a mindful decision-making framework that includes intentional steps. This could involve setting clear objectives, gathering relevant information, considering alternatives, and evaluating the decision's alignment with your values. Mindful decision-making emphasizes a thoughtful and deliberate approach.

7. Mindful Spending Practices:

- Apply mindfulness to your spending habits by practicing conscious consumption. Before making a purchase, pause to consider whether it aligns with your values and financial goals. Mindful spending involves choosing quality over quantity and cultivating gratitude for what you have.

8. Non-Judgmental Observation:

- Cultivate non-judgmental observation of your financial behaviors and patterns. Instead of criticizing yourself for past decisions, observe them without judgment. This approach encourages self-compassion and empowers you to make positive changes moving forward.

9. Mindful Money Check-Ins:

- Schedule regular mindful money check-ins to review your financial goals, progress, and challenges. During these check-ins, practice mindfulness by staying present and fully engaged in the process. Adjust your financial strategies based on changing circumstances or priorities.

10. **Mindful Goal Setting:**

- Set financial goals mindfully by ensuring they align with your values and contribute to your overall well-being. Mindful goal setting involves considering both short-term and long-term objectives and acknowledging the impact of your goals on various aspects of your life.

11. **Gratitude Practices:**

- Integrate gratitude practices into your financial decision-making. Regularly express gratitude for your financial blessings, acknowledging the positive aspects of your financial situation. This practice fosters a mindset of abundance and contentment.

12. **Mindful Planning for the Future:**

- Mindfully plan for the future by considering the long-term consequences of your financial decisions. Whether it's saving for retirement, investing, or making major purchases, mindfulness helps you make choices that contribute to your financial security and well-being.

13. **Mindful Communication:**

- Practice mindful communication about finances with family members, partners, or financial advisors. Approach financial discussions with openness, active listening, and empathy. Mindful communication strengthens relationships and facilitates collaborative decision-making.

By integrating these mindfulness techniques into your decision-making process, you can create a more intentional and balanced approach to your financial well-being. Mindfulness empowers you to make choices aligned with your values, reduces stress associated with financial decisions, and contributes to a more fulfilling and mindful financial life.

Practical steps to develop a sustainable and mindful approach to managing money

Developing a sustainable and mindful approach to managing money involves adopting intentional practices that prioritize long-term financial well-being and align with personal values. Here are practical steps to cultivate a sustainable and mindful approach to money management:

1. **Clarify Financial Values:**

   - Begin by identifying and clarifying your financial values. Reflect on what matters most to you in terms of money and how it aligns with your broader life goals. Understanding your values forms the foundation for making mindful financial decisions.

2. Create a Mindful Budget:

- Develop a budget that reflects your financial values and priorities. Allocate funds intentionally to categories that align with your goals and values, such as savings, debt repayment, and experiences. Regularly review and adjust the budget as needed.

3. Practice Mindful Spending:

- Adopt mindful spending habits by consciously evaluating each purchase. Before making a transaction, consider whether it contributes to your well-being and aligns with your values. Mindful spending involves making intentional choices that bring value and satisfaction.

4. Build an Emergency Fund:

- Establish and maintain an emergency fund as a mindful financial safety net. This fund provides a sense of security and resilience in the face of unexpected expenses, reducing financial stress and enabling more deliberate decision-making.

5. Set Realistic Financial Goals:

- Define realistic and achievable financial goals that align with your values. Break down larger objectives into smaller, manageable steps. Setting realistic goals fosters a sense of accomplishment and motivates sustained financial efforts.

6. Practice Delayed Gratification:

- Cultivate the habit of delayed gratification by pausing before making impulsive purchases. Instead of succumbing to immediate desires, give yourself time to consider the necessity and alignment with your values. Delaying gratification enhances mindfulness and reduces impulse spending.

7. Invest Mindfully:

- Approach investing with a mindful mindset. Understand your risk tolerance, long-term objectives, and the impact of your investments on your overall financial plan. Regularly review your investment portfolio and make adjustments based on your evolving financial goals.

8. **Regular Financial Check-Ins:**

- Schedule regular financial check-ins to assess your progress, celebrate achievements, and address challenges. These check-ins provide a structured opportunity for mindful reflection on your financial journey and enable course corrections as needed.

9. **Conscious Debt Management:**

- Manage debt consciously by understanding the implications of borrowing and making informed decisions. Prioritize debt repayment strategies and avoid accumulating unnecessary debt. Mindful debt management contributes to financial stability and peace of mind.

10. **Cultivate a Mindful Relationship with Money:**

- Develop a mindful and positive relationship with money by reframing negative beliefs and fostering gratitude for your financial resources. Cultivate an abundance mindset that focuses on what you have rather than what you lack.

11. Educate Yourself Mindfully:

   - Approach financial education with mindfulness. Continuously educate yourself about personal finance, investing, and economic trends. Choose resources that align with your learning style and prioritize understanding over following trends.

12. Practice Sustainable Living:

   - Extend mindfulness to your lifestyle choices by embracing sustainability. Consider the environmental and social impact of your purchases and lifestyle. Sustainable living aligns with mindful financial choices that prioritize long-term well-being.

13. Build a Supportive Community:

   - Surround yourself with a supportive community that shares similar financial values. Engage in discussions with friends, family, or online communities that foster positive financial habits and provide encouragement on your mindful financial journey.

14. **Give Mindfully:**

- Incorporate mindful giving into your financial plan. Allocate funds for charitable contributions that align with your values and make a positive impact. Mindful giving fosters a sense of purpose and connection to broader societal well-being.

15. **Regularly Reflect on Your Progress:**

- Set aside time for regular reflection on your financial progress. Celebrate achievements, acknowledge challenges, and adjust your approach as needed. Mindful reflection enhances self-awareness and supports continuous improvement.

By implementing these practical steps, you can cultivate a sustainable and mindful approach to managing money. This intentional mindset fosters financial well-being, reduces stress, and allows you to make decisions that align with your values and long-term goals.

CONCLUSION

As we conclude this exploration into The Psychology of Money: Why Your Brain Controls Your Wallet, I invite you to reflect on the intricate interplay between the mind and finances. Throughout this journey, we've delved into the depths of human psychology, unravelling the evolutionary roots, emotional landscapes, and cognitive biases that shape our financial decisions.

Understanding the psychological underpinnings of money is not merely an academic pursuit; it's a pathway to personal empowerment and financial well-being. We've witnessed how our brains, wired by millennia of evolution, influence our spending habits, investment choices, and overall relationship with money.

Yet, this journey is not one of deterministic inevitability. Instead, it's an invitation to mindfulness—a call to conscious awareness in every financial choice we make. We've explored the transformative potential of cultivating a mindful money mindset, where intentionality, gratitude, and values guide our financial decisions.

As you close the pages of this book, I hope that you carry forward the insights gained into your daily life. Whether you find resonance in the evolutionary roots that govern our instincts, the emotional roller coaster of decision-making, or the cognitive biases that shape our judgments, each revelation contributes to a more informed and empowered relationship with money.

Remember, financial well-being is not measured solely by the numbers in your account, but by the alignment of your financial choices with your authentic self. By acknowledging the psychology behind the dollars and cents, you step into a realm of conscious decision-making—one where your brain becomes an ally rather than a mysterious force controlling your wallet.

May the wisdom within these pages guide you towards financial empowerment, mindful abundance, and a life where your values and your wallet walk hand in hand? The Psychology of Money is an ongoing journey—one that extends beyond these words, inviting you to explore the infinite landscape of your financial psychology with curiosity, awareness, and a profound understanding of the intricate dance between your brain and your wallet.

Thank you for embarking on this transformative exploration. May your financial journey be not only prosperous but also deeply fulfilling, reflective of the values that truly matter to you?